IRISH EMIGRATION
1 8 0 1 - 1 9 2 1

DAVID FITZPATRICK

Printed by
DUNDALGAN PRESS (W. Tempest) LTD.

ISSN No. 0 790-2913
ISBN No. 0 947897 00 3

First Published 1984
Reprinted 1985
,,   1990

INTRODUCTION

Ireland under the Union was a land which most people wanted to leave. At least eight million men, women and children actually did emigrate between 1801 and 1921, a number equal to the entire Irish population at its peak, just before the Great Famine. Members of most generations born during the nineteenth century were more likely than not to move country, so that emigration became part of the expected cycle of life. No other country lost so large a proportion of its people during the century, or experienced such consistently heavy emigration over so long a period. Clearly, movement on such a scale could not have occurred without the combination of powerful foreign demand for immigrant labour and the chronic lack of employment opportunities at home. Nor could it have happened without the creation of complex mechanisms for funding, publicising and implementing emigration. Part I of this study provides a profile of those who left, while Part II analyses the factors facilitating and impeding emigration, ending with a discussion of its fundamental determinants.

Emigration was also one of the great formative factors in modern Irish history. Without studying emigration, one could scarcely hope to explain Ireland's peculiar blend of archaism and modernity as manifested in its economy, demography, social structure and political culture. Majority emigration means, moreover, that the study of Irish history must not be limited to Ireland. If the residual population which stayed at home was not exactly freakish ('the poor, the weak, the old, the lame, the sick, the blind, the dumb, and the imbecile and insane', as Sir William Wilde described it in 1864),[1] neither was it a fair sample of the Irish people. These consequences are explored in Part III. The intention of this pamphlet is thus not only to analyse the profile and determinants of a major historical process, but also to open a neglected window upon the broader vista of Irish history.

1

What follows is largely a synthesis of many specialist studies of social, economic and demographic history. Some of these studies are cited in the Select Bibliography, to which readers should refer when confronted by the name of an author given in capital letters. Otherwise, citations are limited to cases of direct quotation. Many assertions, however, are based upon my own statistical analyses, details of which cannot be given here. Wherever possible, I have excluded numbers from the text, though some have got in by the back door in the guise of diagrams and maps. The few technical terms employed are marked by an asterisk and explained in the Glossary. This essay would have been less readable and less accurate than it is, but for the penetrating scrutiny of David Dickson, Georgina Fitzpatrick, Cormac Ó Gráda, Peter Roebuck and Maryann Gialanella Valiulis. But my primary debt is to eight million others.

Part I: PROFILE

You can emigrate for nothing, boys,
You can emigrate for nothing;
And when your daily toil is done,
You'll write to tell your friends at home
To emigrate for nothing.
Then do not fear the tempest's roar,
Though it were ten times stronger;
But gather up your little store,
Don't wait a moment longer.[2]

Heavy migration was by no means a novelty in nineteenth-century Ireland. Much of Ireland, particularly Ulster, had experienced savage convulsions of population as the result of plantation, transplantation and devastation. During the eighteenth century large numbers of northerners had also crossed the Atlantic. Movement was sporadic and at first affected only a restricted region of Ireland, but towards the end of the century numerous southern Catholics as well as northern Presbyterians were making for America. Transatlantic movement was impeded by war, but resumed on a larger scale soon after the peace settlements of 1815. Over the next three decades well over a million emigrants left Ireland, which quickly became established as the major supplier of overseas labour to both Britain and America. Emigration peaked during the decade 1846-55, when about two and a half millions left the country in response to the Famine and to the social revolution which followed. Thereafter emigration continued at a rate* only slightly lower until the First World War, another four million people being transferred to more congenial environments. As Figure 1 suggests, emigration was subject to short-term and cyclical fluctuation, but lulls such as that for 1876-78 represent postponement rather than abandonment of the decision to emigrate. Even world war and the subsequent legislative restrictions upon immigration could not permanently staunch the 'haemorrhage'.

3

FIGURE 1. IRISH OVERSEAS EMIGRATION, 1825-1915
NUMBER LEAVING THE UNITED KINGDOM PER ANNUM

Statistics refer to Irish-born passengers leaving United Kingdom ports for destinations outside Europe and the Mediterranean. Precise criteria were altered several times, and the graph is most useful as a guide to short-term and cyclical fluctuations. *Source:* Commission on Emigration, Reports (1955), 314-16, with correction of erroneous returns up to 1842.

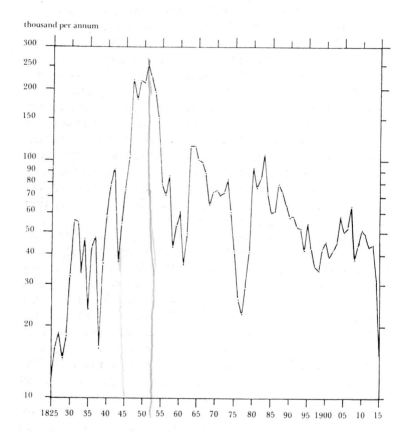

The newly created Irish states proved no better able to provide for their peoples than Ireland had done under the Union. Virtually every English-speaking country experienced extensive Irish settlement, and smaller Irish clusters also developed in Latin America and elsewhere. By the second half of the nineteenth century, enough governments had become interested in the ethnic origins of their inhabitants to enable us to survey the distribution of the world's Irish population. Around 1890 only three-fifths of those born in Ireland were still at home, with three millions living overseas. The United States contained nearly two-thirds of the overseas Irish and one-quarter of all Irish natives. Just after the Famine, however, half the Irish expatriates were living in other countries, including three-quarters of a million in Britain (see Figure 2). At different periods Canada and Australasia each accounted for about one-tenth of the Irish overseas, and in 1870 the Irish were relatively less numerous in the United States than in Scotland, Ontario, New Brunswick, New Zealand and Australia. Many societies apart from Ireland and the United States were affected by the great emigration, and left their imprint upon the settlers.

Irish migration did not conform to any simple 'law' (such as that propounded by RAVENSTEIN) linking probability of migration with proximity of destination. More migrants crossed the Irish Sea than moved county within Ireland, and far more crossed the Atlantic than merely the Irish Sea. Birthplace census returns between 1841 and 1911 show that about half a million Irish residents were usually living outside their native counties, two-thirds of them having merely crossed county borders in search of work or spouses. The Dublin and Belfast regions accounted for between 88 and 99 per cent of net migratory inflow*, and even during the Famine period few inter-county migrants seem to have drifted into the country towns. In general the intensity of internal migration and rural-urban movement was low compared with that in nineteenth-century Britain.

Return migration was also fairly rare. It is true that throughout the century certain coastal regions in the north-west supplied seasonal workers for farmers and contractors in

FIGURE 2.   MIGRATORY IRISH-BORN POPULATION, 1851-1911:
PERCENTAGE DISTRIBUTION BY PLACE OF RESIDENCE, DISTINGUISHING
FOUR COUNTRIES AND IRISH RESIDENTS LIVING OUTSIDE THEIR NATIVE
COUNTY

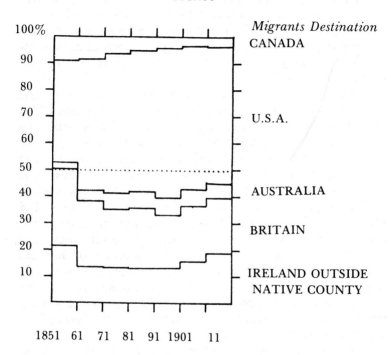

Statistics are drawn from birthplace returns for each region using the census most proximate to the first year of each decade. Australian figures for 1851-71 involve estimation. Statistics exclude outlying islands (Britain), outlying territories in British North America, and minor countries of Irish settlement such as New Zealand, South Africa and Argentina. *Source:* Census of the Irish Free State, 1926; national censuses.

Britain, and before the Famine as many as one hundred thousand migrants annually plied back and forth across the Irish Sea. But reverse migration* from the United States, though sometimes considerable in recession years such as the late 1850s and mid-1870s, was probably less common among the Irish than among almost any other ethnic group by the early twentieth century. GOULD'S calculations suggest that for every hundred Irish emigrants (excluding temporary visitors) only about 6 returned from the United States, compared with 12 English, 22 German or 58 Italian settlers. Irish emigrants tended to go far and not come back.

The profile of Irish emigration deviated in several respects from that of the other great nineteenth-century migrations. Men usually dominated migration from Europe, yet in the Irish case women were equally migratory. Studies by ERICKSON, Ó GRÁDA and MOKYR show that, even before the Famine, two-fifths of Irish emigrants to north America were female. Thereafter men predominated only for a brief period about 1870, and women had the majority just after the Famine and towards the end of the century. The balance of sexes seldom strayed far from parity, even for particular counties of origin or particular regions of settlement. Women formed a small majority of internal migrants, and about the turn of the century they were less likely than men to settle in the British dominions rather than the United States. In general, however, massive emigration did not result in major distortion of the sex ratio, either for the Irish overseas or for the residual population at home.

Parity of sexes was rendered all the more remarkable by the relative insignificance of family movement in the Irish case. Most European migrations were comprised of a blend of family groups and unaccompanied men; Irish emigrants were less inclined to travel in family groups and more likely to be unattached women. During the quarter-century leading up to the Famine, only about half of the Irish emigrants landing at Boston and New York travelled in family groups. Family emigration probably peaked during the late 1840s, and seems to have declined steadily in importance between the Famine and the First World War. By 1906-14 married people accounted for only one-tenth of Irish emigrants. This trend was reflected in the proportion of children under 15 years, which fell from one-quarter to one-twelfth over the period. Emigrants to the British dominions were more likely to travel in family groups than those to the United States, but everywhere the Irish emigrant was more likely than his British counterpart to be an unmarried adult.

The preponderance of unmarried adults among Irish emigrants is reflected in the age-structure of those leaving. Before the Famine about two-thirds of those travelling to north America were young adults aged under 35. During the period 1855-1914, the proportion of Irish emigrants aged between 20 and 24 ranged from one-third to 44 per cent, the proportion peaking about 1900. Figure 3 illustrates both the even balance of sexes and the impressive concentration in the narrow age-band of those who had just entered the employment market and were about to enter the marriage market. It indicates that post-Famine emigration was integrated into the life-cycle of both sexes, tending to occur soon after maturity or never. Girls emigrated (or married) rather earlier than boys, but for both sexes the probability of emigration declined sharply after the age of 30 with only a tiny proportion of 50-year-olds venturing out of Ireland. Emigration was a young man's — and a young woman's — game.

The great majority of emigrants seem to have left Ireland without marketable skills. Most were returned in shipping lists and official statistics as mere 'servants' or 'labourers', occupational labels which expressed hope more often than accomplishment since many left in search of their first paid employment. Even before the Famine, only a minority of men claimed higher status than labourer while even fewer female emigrants aspired beyond domestic service. Later in the century the proportions of labourers and servants seldom fell below four-fifths, always far exceeding the proportions for emigrants from Britain. At first certain skilled trades were over-represented by comparison with the home population, but textile workers, like farmers and professional people, were disinclined to emigrate. The Irish exodus cannot plausibly be depicted as a movement of redundant artisans, still less as a draining away of 'human capital'.

Apart from their occupational homogeneity, Irish emigrants were probably as innumerate and illiterate as the populations from which they sprang. Most of those who left were virtually unencumbered by training, expertise or accomplishment. They emerged from a context of enforced idleness and ignorance full of eagerness to learn how to labour and to serve. Statistical evidence of the counties of origin of the emigrants is incomplete and inconsistent. The most satisfactory indirect measure for *net* outward migration is probably 'cohort depletion'*. As Figure 4 illustrates, the basic regional distribution was already established during the Famine decade of the 1840s. Earlier emigration had been most intensive from northern and midlands counties, but from the Famine onwards depletion tended to be greatest in the Connaught region, with a gradual extension of heavy emigration down the length of the western seaboard. Broadly speaking, emigration was heavier from poorer and more agricultural counties, being relatively light from the more anglicized and commercialized south-east and north-east. Though these crude calculations tell us nothing of local contrasts or of the social status of emigrants within their own counties, they cast doubt upon the influential thesis of COUSENS, who claimed that the correlation between poverty and heavy emigration was a novelty of the last quarter of the century. From the 1840s onwards, emigration was not only intensive from virtually every county but also most heavily concentrated in the regions of greatest poverty and least off-farm employment.

It is not practicable in this brief profile of a century's migration to analyse regional variations in the composition and direction of movement. It may however be shown that female majorities were most common among emigrants from Connaught and the north midlands, while from the 1880s onwards the largest proportions of children and married emigrants came from the more prosperous eastern counties. Just after the Famine, however, heavy child emigration had also affected western counties such as Galway, Kerry and Cork, as cottiers and small farmers escaped with their families. Less is known about regional contrasts in occupations, but just before the First World War

FIGURE 3.　EMIGRATION FROM IRISH PORTS, MAY 1851-1914:
PERCENTAGE DISTRIBUTION BY SEX, DISTINGUISHING EMIGRANTS
AGED 20-24, FOR EACH QUINQUENNIUM

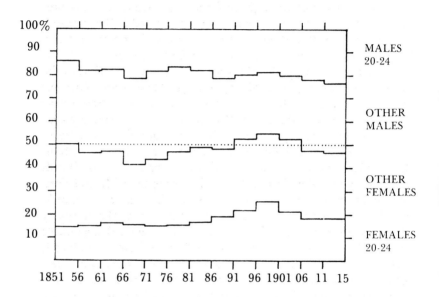

Statistics for the first quinquennium (1851-55) exclude the period January-April 1851, and those for the last (1911-15) exclude the wartime year of 1915. Returns for the age-group 20-24 have been adjusted for non-specification of age. *Source:* Annual returns published in Census of Ireland, 1851-1911; Agricultural Statistics, 1856-75; Emigration Statistics, 1876-1914.

emigrants from Leinster and especially Ulster were less likely than those from Munster or Connaught to be labourers and more likely to be farmers or artisans.

There were also spectacular contrasts in the regional origins of emigrants choosing different destinations, suggesting the existence of distinct 'streams' of emigration. Statistics for the period 1876-1914 show that American emigrants were most likely to emanate from Connaught and the west, whereas Canadians were concentrated in Ulster and the north. 'Permanent' emigrants to Scotland tended to come from the north-east and those to England from eastern and southern coastal regions, but 'seasonal' migrants to Britain were increasingly clustered in the north-western counties of Mayo, Donegal, Galway and Roscommon. Since English birthplace statistics for 1911 show heavy representation for Mayo and Roscommon, it seems likely that many of these 'seasonal' workers in fact lingered on in Britain. The antipodean movement was also distinctive. The Australian-Irish tended to come from south-western and north midlands counties, while New Zealand, with its strong Scottish tradition, attracted emigrants from Ulster as well. These contrasts should not be exaggerated, for the United States was the majority destination for emigrants from almost every county. Recognisable local links developed between Waterford and Newfoundland, Wexford and Argentina, Clare and Australia, Kerry and New Zealand, Derry and Philadelphia. But these localized axes were swamped statistically by the mighty migratory scattering which mixed up virtually every county of origin with virtually every destination.

These disparities in regional origin were associated with important differences in the social composition of the various emigrant streams. I have suggested elsewhere that many Irish emigrants to Britain (though not the seasonal 'harvesters') may plausibly be characterised as townsmen circulating in the wider urban employment market of the British Isles. The American-Irish, though also bound for urban employment abroad, were drawn from the surplus of a rural population which had formerly subsisted upon potato production before the coming of the blight. Emigrants to Australia, if a fair sample of their native

FIGURE 4.   COHORT DEPLETION, 1821-1911

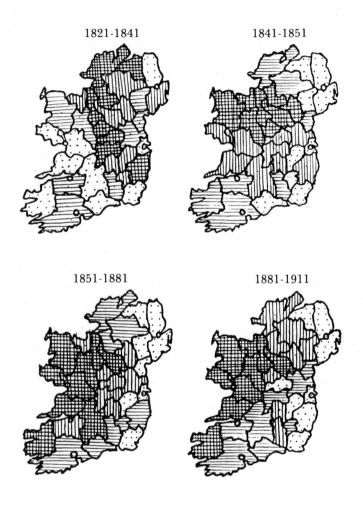

These maps show the proportion of the cohort initially aged 5-24 which 'disappeared' over the subsequent decade. The third and fourth maps represent average figures over three decades, and the first map refers to depletion over a twenty-year period of the cohort initially aged 6-15. Counties are ranked in descending order of depletion, the first eight being marked by cross-hatching, ranks 9-16 by verticals, ranks 17-24 by horizontals and ranks 25-32 by dots. *Source:* Census of Ireland, 1821-1911.

populations, were more likely to be semi-skilled farm workers rendered unemployable by the rapid contraction of tillage farming in such counties as Clare, Limerick and Tipperary. The available statistics of occupation suggest that all major emigrant streams were dominated by young, unmarried adults listed as labourers or servants. Towards the end of the century those choosing Australasia or Canada were rather more likely than emigrants to the United States to diverge from stereotype by claiming higher occupational status or travelling in family groups. The reverse probably applied during the Famine period, when the criteria for assistance to Australia and the cheapness of tickets to Canada tended to draw those who were unskilled and unattached to colonial ports. The religious professions of emigrants were not systematically recorded, though from the 1840s onwards most were certainly Catholics. Nevertheless, Protestants made up about two-thirds of the Irish population of Ontario through most of the century, and also contributed heavily to Irish settlement in Scotland, New Zealand and Pennsylvania. They accounted for about one-fifth of state-assisted Irish emigrants to New South Wales, roughly the proportion expected from their county distribution of origins. Variations in social composition had some influence upon the subsequent performance of Irish settlers in different countries, yet the structure of the host societies was a far more important factor (see Part III). To alien eyes and ears, it often mattered little whether an Irish emigrant was from Dublin or Mayo, a Protestant or a Catholic, a labourer or an artisan, a parent or on the loose. To their great indignation, the Irish overseas tended to be lumped together as ignorant, dirty and primitive Paddies or Biddies.

Part II: DETERMINANTS

My father was a farming man, used to industry,
He had two sons to manhood grown, and lovely daughters three,
Our acres few that would not do, so some of us must roam,
With sisters two I bade adieu to Erin's lovely home.
My father sold his second cow, and borrowed twenty pounds,
And in the pleasant month of May we sailed from Sligo town;
With hundreds more we left the shore, all oblidged to roam
My heart dose break when this I speak of Erin's lovely home.[3]

To the nineteenth-century mind, if not the Irish nationalist mind, emigration seemed a Good Thing. It was a commonplace of political economy that free international movement of labour should be facilitated in order to reduce regional disparities in the balance between capital and labour. Yet there was no consensus among economists or politicians as to the desirability of subsidising emigration, or the extent to which the state should interfere in the selection, transportation, direction and settlement of any recipients of assistance. During the century after Waterloo the state did not try to restrict emigration from Ireland, except to prevent the flight of criminals or the dumping of Irish paupers on British parishes. But positive interference in emigration was another matter. Most economists concurred that pre-Famine Ireland suffered from chronic 'overpopulation', but they disagreed as to the practicability of curing the disease by emigration. The underlying problem was widely believed to be a combination of insufficient capital and inefficient exploitation of land. Early in the century many economists, including Malthus and McCulloch, argued that assistance for emigration was a palliative rather than a cure, and an expensive palliative at that. Both writers later endorsed state assistance at moments and locations of particular crisis, provided that it was complemented by measures to promote farm consolidation and capital investment. Less qualified advocacy came from Senior and Whately, who unavailingly urged introduction of state-funded emigration rather than workhouse relief during the 1830s.

14

The effect of recurrent scarcity and finally famine was to concentrate the attention of economists and politicians upon immediate remedies rather than enduring solutions. Westminster politicians paid more heed to the Irish landlord lobby, led by Monteagle and Godley, and the various groups advocating systematic colonization associated with Horton, Wakefield and Torrens. The growing political consensus in favour of the principle of assistance was manifested in numerous reports of royal commissions and select committees, and even in prime-ministerial plans. But principled approval was too feeble a sentiment to generate massive provision of public funds. From 1848 onwards the sense of urgency receded, largely because the extension of private emigration seemed to render state assistance unnecessary. Thereafter theoretical approval of quality-controlled emigration under state supervision remained widespread, but only occasionally were practical efforts made to implement it. Parsimonious politicians preferred uncontrolled but self-financed emigration, and left it to the governments of receiving countries to impose restrictions upon the quality of immigrants. Economic theory played only a marginal part in shaping Irish emigration.

Within Ireland, the strongest advocacy of controlled emigration came from landlords and their agents. Before the Famine they found their estates increasingly cluttered with squatters, small holders and their surplus children. These 'redundant' inhabitants generated little or no income for the proprietor, threatened to become charges on the estate as pensioners or paupers, and constituted a turbulent element in society. Their presence also made socially impracticable the fundamental restructuring of estates of which many 'progressive' or 'improving' proprietors dreamed. Many landlords therefore advocated removal of entire family units to distant destinations, until the 'optimum' population for estate reform had been reached. Like politicians, landlords found it easier to advocate assistance than to provide it. Indeed the political focus of the emigration question was its funding rather than its desirability, with government and gentry each trying to manoeuvre the other party into paying the bills. The Famine increased both the urgency of the 'overpopulation' problem and the possibility of carrying out estate reform, and a number of proprietors acted upon their own advice. But post-Famine depopulation and stabilization reversed both trends, and soon most landlords were content to exercise their declining influence upon that part of the population which chose to stay behind.

Theoretical objections to emigration were no more effective in stopping the exodus than was theoretical approval in promoting it. Before the Famine nationalists tended to regard emigration with distaste, as an ugly by-product of misgovernment which would right itself once an Irish Parliament had been given the opportunity to solve Ireland's problems of land tenure and capital. In 1845 O'Connell strongly rejected 'the notion of there being a surplus population', protesting 'that it seems to be taken for granted that man is a nuisance'. Emigration was 'not a remedy', since the places of emigrants were 'filled with great rapidity'.[4] Yet nationalists were inconsistent. O'Connell had urged state assistance in 1837, and Smith O'Brien (himself a landed proprietor) was among the most energetic advocates of state colonization as a means of coping with Irish poverty. From the Famine onwards nationalist rhetoric hardened against encouragement of emigration, which was now firmly linked with 'clearances' and 'extermination'. Internal migration was feebly proposed as an alternative, and Parnell himself was associated with an unsuccessful commercial venture to transplant 'congests' to estates cleared for the purpose. Parnell soon lost his faith in internal migration, but remained adamant that state-funded family emigration would 'leave us none but the old men and the old women, that would be one way of dealing with the Irish question, certainly'.[5]

The Catholic clergy followed a parallel path from inconsistency to rhetorical condemnation. Before the Famine Fr. Mathew, Bishop Doyle and other influential churchmen had supported certain forms of emigration and even state assistance. Once continuous depopulation began, clerical condemnation became more strident as priests grew alarmed at the demoralization — and depletion — of their congregations. Yet emigration had its compensations for the Church. Undeniably, it raised countless thousands from domestic degradation and poverty to a decent livelihood overseas, and seemed as beneficient to the individual as it was deemed harmful to society. Moreover it promoted the rapid growth of Catholicism (and Irish nationalism) in Britain and the New World. As P. A. SHEEHAN, later novelist and canon, exclaimed in 1882: 'Well, God's will be done! God knoweth best! We cheerfully made the sacrifice, and behold our reward! The exiles have prospered. The 3,000,000 have grown to 10,000,000'. In practice, the clergy suspended their scruples in individual cases. Virtually every parish priest in the west of Ireland participated in Vere Foster's scheme of assistance for female emigration during the early 1880s. A number of clergymen in Ireland as well as America promoted schemes for 'Catholic colonization' in Minnesota and elsewhere. Clerical opposition to emigration was largely directed against evicting landlords who preferred 'cattle to Christians', and state assistance of family emigration which tended 'only to promote disaffection amongst the Irish race at home and abroad'.[6] For its opponents as much as its advocates, the massive fact of emigration outweighed and enfeebled the expression of mere opinion.

Thus theories and ideologies colouring the thought of public men did little to shape the character or intensity of Irish emigration. This gulf between reality and precept fostered ambivalence in the attitudes of economists, politicians, landlords, nationalists and priests alike, so undermining whatever influence their attitudes might otherwise have had upon the decisions of the potential emigrants themselves. As one bishop replied when asked if he were opposed to emigration: 'I am, and I am not';[7] small wonder that the Irish people listened to their mentors, and did not listen. To isolate the determinants of emigrant decisions, one must explore the material factors facilitating and impeding emigration, and beyond that investigate its underlying causes.

State financial assistance to emigrants was intermittent and localized, veering between the prodigal and the miserly. The first major scheme was undertaken in 1823 and 1825 under Peter Robinson, who removed over 2,300 people in family groups from a dozen Munster estates to Canada. The scheme was designed to relieve not only land hunger but also agrarian discontent and outrage. Both emigrants and estates were adjudged to have benefited, but the cost (£20 a head) appalled contemporaries, and future assistance seldom exceeded £5. Large-scale assistance resumed during the Famine, when 4,000 female orphans were shipped from workhouses to woman-hungry Australia and 1,000 turbulent inhabitants of Crown estates were despatched to America. Boards of Guardians were also enabled to borrow on the security of the rates in order to contribute to the emigration of paupers and potential paupers. Under these powers nearly 45,000 emigrants were helped to Canada and elsewhere between 1849 and 1906. The last major project was that of 1883-91, when over 25,000 westerners were helped out of scheduled 'distressed districts' with a combination of state, local and philanthropic aid. Official funds were also used, mainly earlier in the century, to emigrate special categories such as military pensioners, Crown witnesses and convicts. Of these groups only the last was transported involuntarily, though cries of genocide and depopulation were constantly raised by critics of the state.

Official assistance from colonial and foreign funds was of greater importance. In the Australian case alone, most Irish settlers received some form of government subsidy. Costs were generally met from colonial land funds, often supplemented by personal remittances, but until late in the century transportation was handled either by private 'bounty' contractors or by the Emigration Commissioners. By about 1872, when the Commissioners surrendered their functions to the Board of Trade and central supervision of assisted movement to Australia ceased, 140,000 Irish emigrants had been assisted to the Australian colonies in addition to forty or fifty thousand convicts. During the 1870s the New Zealand government brought out about 20,000 Irish settlers, while incentives such as land grants, shipping subsidies and internal transport facilities were occasionally made available in Canada, South Africa, certain American states and territories, and some Latin American countries. Excluding indirect and punitive assistance as well as Australasian aid after 1872, at least 32,000 emigrants

received state help between 1818 and 1845, 16,000 between 1846
and 1850, and 170,000 between 1851 and 1906. Thus most state
aid was provided when it was least needed and least widely
urged, that is after the Famine. A few schemes, such as
Robinson's in the 1820s and the Local Government Board's in
the 1880s, applied theory by removing entire households and
so facilitating consolidation of farms and long-term 'deconges-
tion'. But the great majority of assisted as well as unassisted
emigrants comprised surplus offspring whose removal was
thought to benefit the society they settled in as much as that
which they left. State aid was crucial in shaping Irish movement
to Australasia, significant in the Canadian case, but otherwise
of negligible importance.

Private benefactors were even less munificent than the state
in funding systematic emigration. Analysis of a wide range of
official and private sources indicates that between 1826 and 1889
some private assistance was provided in every county, being
concentrated in Leinster and Munster before the Famine,
Leinster and Connaught during the Famine and Connaught and
Munster thereafter. At least 180 landlords and philanthropists
offered some form of assistance to more than 80,000 emigrants.
Of these 23,000 received small but essential subsidies from Vere
Foster's fund for getting girls out of Ireland. Also in the early
1880s, 10,000 impoverished westerners were removed under the
supervision of the Quaker banker, James Hack Tuke, funding
being shared between the state and 'Mr. Tuke's Committee'.

Otherwise, the bulk of assisted emigration was conducted
by ten major landlords, who sent out 30,000 emigrants in
batches ranging between one and six thousand per landlord.
In roughly descending order of 'munificence', these benefactors were as follows: Fitzwilliam (Wicklow), Wandesforde
(Kilkenny), Lansdowne (Kerry and Queen's), Bath (Monaghan),
Palmerston (Sligo), Wyndham (Clare and Limerick), Gore Booth
(Sligo), Spaight (Clare and Tipperary), de Vesci (Queen's) and
Mahon (Roscommon). Most of them had extensive landed or
mercantile interests outside their Irish estates, which enabled
them to raise cash even when rent was unpaid and the need for
emigration seemed correspondingly urgent. Several landlords

also exploited state funds in order to relieve congestion on their estates. Lord Monteagle, the influential politician and advocate of colonization, sent numerous tenants and dependants from Limerick to Australia using a combination of state assistance and generous personal loans, which were often punctiliously repaid. Emigration sponsored by landlords was usually conducted in an humane if not extravagant spirit. Demand for assistance normally exceeded supply, and the recipients gave voice to gratitude more often than resentment. Forced emigration was rare, in the restricted sense that those few landlords who provided passage money seldom offered their tenants the bleak choice of emigration or destitution. But assistance was an act of business rather than philanthropy, and on the Fitzwilliam estate families without separate houses were refused passages on the ground that their removal would not facilitate consolidation of holdings.

The pattern of private benefaction over time reflected changes in landlord mentality. The sense that Irish estates were capable of being reorganised as profitable business enterprises was largely confined to the Famine period and the subsequent phase of traffic in encumbered estates. Likewise, investment in emigration was concentrated in the period 1840-60. Apart from those aided by Tuke and Vere Foster, at least 12,000 emigrants seem to have been assisted privately between 1826 and 1845, 22,000 between 1846 and 1850, and perhaps 14,000 thereafter. In addition, a great but unknown number of tenants was indirectly assisted through compensation for surrender, permission to sell tenant interest, or the 'forgiving' of rent arrears. In the context of a society clamouring for resources to fund emigration, landlords deserved censure not for pursuing a 'policy of extermination', but for devoting so little of their income to improving the survival chances of their dependants by helping them out of the country.

The assistance offered by state, landlords and philanthropists was dwarfed by that sent home by emigrants to their families. Throughout the nineteenth century the state made available less than £400,000 in subsidies and loans, together with something over £1,100,000 from colonial funds in support of emigration to Australia. The cost of recorded systematic assistance from private sources may not have exceeded £500,000. By contrast official returns revealed that over £34,000,000 was sent to the United Kingdom by north American emigrants between 1848 and 1887, the bulk of it going to Ireland. Though much 'American money' was used in payment of rent, shop debts and farm purchase, two-fifths of the remittances came in the form of pre-paid passage tickets. It seems certain that the great majority of Irish emigrants owed their basic passage money to their predecessors.

Already in the 1830s Irish movement out of the British Isles was widely believed to be a 'chain migration', whereby the selection of future emigrants lay largely with those who had gone before. Their patterns of preference clarify the functions of emigration within the family unit. The Canadian-Irish of the early 1840s, mostly of northern Protestant origin, were more inclined to send remittances to wives and parents than to siblings (though siblings received larger amounts than parents and males were preferred to females). A rather different chain was established between nominators in Victoria and their Irish beneficiaries (mainly southern Catholics) between 1856 and 1861. Three-quarters of nominees were of the same generation (compared with 44 per cent for non-Irish nominations) and males were only marginally preferred. Very few parents were summoned, and the Irish were unusually prone to select 'friends' or distant connections. Above all, the Australian-Irish were remarkable for the eagerness with which they exploited government nomination schemes, whereby nominators deposited cash on behalf of specified emigrants for whom colonial governments paid most of the passage cost. As in America, Irish settlers were more active in building migration chains than other, usually wealthier, immigrant groups. Chain migration, at first serving to reassemble household units temporarily fractured by the hurried departure of 'pioneers', became the main agency for trans-planting the young adults of each generation. The chain mechanism gradually broadened its function from household to communal replanting.

Thus external funding was crucial in facilitating and moulding Irish emigration. Landlords or the state helped 'pioneer' emigrants escape a few impoverished and 'congested' localities, though most 'overpopulated' districts received no such initial shove. Once extensive emigration from a neighbourhood began, it was largely sustained by the chain mechanism. Thereafter, the function of munificent landlords or guardians was to supplement the basic fare by meeting ancillary expenses. The price range for steerage passages varied surprisingly little during the century, though competition meant that in any one season fares to north America might range between two and six pounds, and those to Australia between ten and fifteen pounds. The passage price covered basic provisioning for the voyage, as required under increasingly rigorous British and American passenger legislation. But even the most parsimonious emigrant normally required a pound or so at each end for transport, board and lodging, and as much again for an 'outfit' of suitable clothing. The unsubsidized cost of one passage to America was thus roughly equivalent to the value of a heifer, or the rent of a typical Mayo farm at the end of the century. It also somewhat exceeded the likely annual savings of a girl lately arrived in the United States. Thus most would-be emigrants could hope at best to cover their own passage rather than that of their households, whether sale of stock and effects or remittance from abroad was to meet the cost. The structure of emigrant financing strongly favoured individual movement, but was flexible enough to enable even paupers to go, provided well-disposed 'pioneers' had gone before them.

Those lacking heifers, furniture, 'goodwill' or generous friends still had a fighting chance of surmounting the obstacles to emigration. The passenger trade was highly competitive, and cheap tickets rewarded those prepared to shop, and wait, about. Irish emigrants proved highly responsive to price variations, which were rapidly broadcast through a dense network of local agencies from the 1820s onwards. Canny Irishmen flocked to Canada rather than the United States when cheaper passages were available up to 1848, and staggered to Liverpool rather than Irish ports in pursuit of bargain fares during the Famine and its immediate sequel. Early in the century, discounts were readily obtainable, since many shippers were grateful to fill their holds with human ballast for the return journey westwards, after depositing their major cargoes of timber, cotton or flaxseed. Specialist emigrant vessels were in service from 1816 onwards, but the fleet was inadequate to cope with demand during the Famine. Subsequently, encouraged first by persistent passenger demand in Europe and later by the growing reverse movement back from the New World, shippers specialized increasingly in the passenger trade. Yet heavy discounts were still available, at least in slack years, as during the 'steamship war' of 1885. Similar factors affected traffic across the Irish Sea, which included not only emigrants to Britain but also millions bound indirectly for the New World. In this case, however, pre-Famine emigrants had to jostle with livestock, since more goods left Irish ports than entered them. But as specialist carriers developed and competed, prices fell. During the heady days of 1849-51, cross-channel shippers vied with each other to take on passengers for a few pence, and even in normal seasons the shorter voyages usually cost less than six shillings.

The cheapness of travel between Ireland and Britain, and between Britain and America, encouraged 'step-wise' migration during much of the century. Impecunious emigrants could walk and beg their way to a sea port, rough it across the Irish Sea, save a few pounds from casual labour in southern Scotland or northern England, and ultimately invest their savings in a transatlantic passage. Many migrants meandered rather than rushed towards the promised land. The case history of Owen Peter Mangan from Co. Cavan illustrates some of the migratory expedients of a penniless Catholic trying to escape post-Famine Ireland.[8] Mangan was born and orphaned just before the Famine, and his mother's precipitate remarriage encouraged the rapid dispersal of his four elder brothers. One brother went to New Orleans after five years as a farm servant; another married in Durham but later departed for Philadelphia to escape arrest as a Fenian. A third brother went to sea, while the fourth left Newry for Philadelphia after a stint with the papal army. Owen himself spent much of his childhood pursuing his elusive mother and step-father across the north of Ireland, cadging sixpences, dinners and coach lifts as he went. After a brief spell in a Drogheda cotton mill in 1853, Mangan made off with three 'chums' to Liverpool and Preston, paying two shillings for the crossing. In England he worked as a cotton weaver, factory operative, policeman and grocer. He married but grew restive as his chums dispersed abroad and as his business faltered. In 1869 he began a new cycle of migration by moving to Philadelphia, and like two of his brothers he had soon saved enough to bring out his family. Mangan's story suggests that rigid distinctions between internal, cross-channel and trans-atlantic migration are artificial. Many individual emigrant lives encompassed them all.

The Irish experience contraverts GOULD's 'diffusion' theory of migration, which predicts the gradual spread of migratory habits in the vicinity of existing centres of intensive migration, as information is diffused and psychic resistance defused. In Ireland a blend of aggressive marketing and popular thirst for information accelerated the diffusion process to the point where it ceases to have ·explanatory value. This is evident in the remarkably even spread of 'cohort depletion' over the 1850s immediately after the Famine-wrought transformation of emigration patterns. More than a quarter of the population aged 5-24 'disappeared' in every county except Dublin, Antrim and Kildare. The comparable figure for England and Wales was under ten per cent.

Universal awareness of the range of emigrant options was helped by the proliferation of shipping sub-agencies among country shopkeepers. Shipping propaganda decorated the walls of cabins and school houses, where concentration upon the geography of every country except Ireland provided further stimulus. The rapid spread of basic literacy after the 1830s was widely believed to be acting as a catalyst, both by enabling the mass of younger people to spell out shipping advertisements in shops and newspapers, and by encouraging awareness of ways of life beyond the parish. But still more important was the institution of the 'American letter', which was often dictated by an illiterate for reading aloud to other illiterates. Apart from money (the most eloquent argument for emigration) the letter would often contain practical details of employment options, wage rates, transport costs, diet and networks of Irish contacts. These facts would be broadcast well beyond the writer's immediate circle, and made emigration seem feasible as well as desirable.

Despite sophisticated networks of information and promotion, the Irish emigration business suffered recurrent setbacks. Fear of shipwreck probably remained powerful long after the triumph of steam in mid-century had made the risk negligible. People were also slow to forget the horrors of 'Black '47' and the 'coffin ships', when infections contracted ashore but rapidly transmitted in the squalid shipboard environment had been mainly responsible for the death of 17,000 of the 100,000 emigrants from the British Isles to Quebec. Of these victims half died aboard ship or in hospital on Grosse Isle, including one-sixth of the Liverpool emigrants and nearly one-fifth of those from Cork. Subsequent tightening of passenger legislation, together with less cursory medical examinations and reduced prevalence of lice-borne fever bacilli, ensured that shipboard mortality seldom reached two per cent after 1847. Significantly, this appalling episode did not stop emigration but merely redirected it towards ports in the United States, a substitution aided by the raising of Canadian port taxes in order to discourage the inflow of Irish paupers. There were of course other dangers than death entailed by emigration. Fraud, imposition and persecution by runners and touts were rife until the 1850s. Moreover the separation of sexes was not always complete, and moralists throughout the century feared for the safety of emigrant females. One Catholic preacher conjured up 'their shrieks for assistance, at the dead of night, rising from the steerage cabin of a foreign ship . . . is there no grief for the ruined virgins of the Emigrant Brothels?'.[9] In the second half of the century, however, such abuses were rare, and even at its height shipboard roguery could not dampen Irish enthusiasm for emigration.

Far more serious in its impact on emigration was recession in the receiving countries. To some extent failure of labour demand in America or Britain could be met by redirection of movement, since the structure of the transatlantic economy after 1850 ensured that the two business cycles moved in opposite phase. But because the United States was by far the largest emigration market, recession there caused major reductions in overall movement out of Ireland during the early 1860s, later 1870s and late 1890s (see Figure 1). Temporary blockage of non-military emigration was also brought about by wartime disruption (before 1815 and after 1915) and by legislative restriction. After about 1885 the United States gradually limited the range of acceptable aliens, but these measures were largely directed against the 'New Immigration' from continental Europe and against 'contract labour', which no longer applied to many Irish newcomers. Even the quota legislation of the 1920s scarcely touched the Irish intake, though other qualitative controls did discourage Irish movement to the United States thereafter. In the Australasian case immigration policy had more pronounced effects, since most Irish emigrants were assisted and since the criteria for assistance were frequently altered. Yet there were enough Australasian colonies to ensure that, for much of the century, most alert emigrants could find some government willing to assist them. In summary, the physical, economic and legislative impediments affected the timing and destination of emigration without much reducing the longer-term outflow. That more profound obstacle to emigration, the obstinate desire to battle it out in one's own country, had been wrenched out of Irish mentality in most neighbourhoods by the end of the Famine. Even in the 'backward' north-west, seasonal migration often provided a preparation for emigration rather than an alternative to it. Ultimately it was this transformation of mentality, more than any calculation of costs and risks, which ensured that the Irish would become an emigrant people.

What caused the 'sea change' in Irish mentality? Without mighty forces at work no network of agencies, no structure of funding, could have induced the majority of most nineteenth-century generations to move country. In 1851 *The Times* sagely observed that 'emigrations commonly begin in repulsion, and go on with attraction'.[10] In a sense this dichotomy is false, since both 'push' and 'pull' are prerequisite to every decision leading to migration. Yet the two factors may usefully be separated in analysis of the timing and destination of movement.

Selection of destination, though limited in range by the amount of resources released as a result of the 'push', largely depended upon informed comparison of the material attractions of different societies. Timing of migration was crucially influenced both by the extent of deprivation in the home context (a subjective concept, depending upon one's expectations), and by the improvement in living standards expected to result from movement overseas. One might expect push factors to predominate in periods of dearth or sudden immiseration, pull factors being more significant when better conditions at home permitted more leisurely calculation of costs and benefits. The strength of the push determined whether or not one could afford to delay emigration in the hope of a stronger pull.

During the two decades before the Famine, 'repulsion' was a powerful factor generating heavy emigration from many classes and localities. The transatlantic pull was as yet feeble by comparison with the second half of the century, when rapid urban and industrial expansion created relentless demand for immigrant labour. But the factors tending to push the Irish out of their homeland were commensurately stronger. Figure 1 shows wild fluctuation from year to year in the level of emigration between 1830 and 1845, reflecting the impact of bad seasons and poor harvests upon a population much of which teetered on the margins of destitution. Peaks in emigration occurred in 1830-32, 1834, 1836-37, and 1841-42; whereas, according to Wilde as summarised by CONNELL, partial failures of the potato crop occurred in 1829-30, 1832-34, 1836, 1839 and 1841-42. Thus a failure in the staple crop was usually closely followed by a sharp increase in emigration. Pre-Famine emigration, already dominated by vulnerable 'labourers' and 'servants', acted as a vital safety-valve in years of distress at home.

This interpretation suggests that Ireland did indeed suffer from the condition of 'overpopulation' so often lamented by observers before the Famine. MOKYR and other recent writers, on the other hand, have suggested that poverty was no more prevalent in pre-Famine Ireland than in several contemporary European societies, and that the marginal product of labour normally exceeded the cost of subsistence. National income *per* capita may actually have been rising, despite the continuing rapid growth of population up to the mid-1840s. It is however likely that the stable or rising level of mean income masked increasing inequality of wealth, with farmers prospering while a deprived class of cottiers and occasional labourers multiplied. The revisionist thesis is also rendered dubious by apparent errors in MOKYR's computations of income and regularity of employment for rural labourers. In many localities, and in bad years, most labourers and children of small farmers could not hope to earn their keep by wages drawn during the brief periods of spring planting or harvest, and their supply of home-grown food was often exhausted before summer. The rarity of death from starvation or malnutrition should be attributed not to absence of poverty, but to provision of relief by relatives, neighbours, or less frequently the state. One form of relief, which became increasingly prevalent during the prelude to the Famine, was emigration.

The impulse to be anywhere but in Ireland was clearly strongest of all during the late 1840s. The Famine, after all, entailed no mere fall in living standards, or 'partial failure' of the crop, but the threat of imminent destitution or death for the bulk of those who had formerly relied upon potato cultivation for their sustenance. The vast increase of pauper emigration during the Famine reflected the vast increase of pauperism. Yet the Famine had an important secondary effect on emigration. It not only drove the destitute to struggle and stumble out of Ireland, but it also persuaded many formerly comfortable farmers to cut their losses by disposing of their depreciating tenant interest and removing their families to America or Britain. It was during the Famine, rather than beforehand or afterwards, that the departing emigrant came to be visualised as the 'bone and sinew' of the nation.

After the mid-1850s the urgency of emigration diminished. Many farm workers remained underemployed and many farmers produced very little surplus over their domestic needs, even in good years. But the overall decline in population, together with gradual diversification of production and diet, ensured that subsistence crises would only occasionally dictate immediate emigration. On the western seaboard, however, high marriage rates, high marital fertility*, and archaic land use meant that both depopulation and diversification were more sluggish than in richer regions where they were less needed. Failure of potato production therefore could still cause acute deprivation, as in 1879, and it is significant that short-term fluctuations in emigration were far sharper in Connaught than elsewhere. In general, though, emigration rates were more uniform than before the Famine, both over time and between counties. Despite S. C. JOHNSON's suggestion to the contrary, no clear negative correlation was now discernible between annual emigration levels and the size of the potato crop. As Figure 1 indicates, the level of emigration after the Famine fluctuated cyclically rather than from year to year. The cyclical peaks in emigration corresponded closely with business 'booms' in the New World, which themselves coincided broadly with recessions in the British Isles. Indeed, THOMAS has argued that transatlantic migration was a major factor in linking together the business cycles of the European and American economies. But from the viewpoint of the young Irish adult, it was the allure of foreign countries rather than the abstract mechanism of the business cycle which determined the timing and direction of emigration. Pull factors became predominant, and migration decisions appear to have been sensitive to regional disparities in employment and perhaps also wage rates. The 'push' out of Ireland no longer depended primarily upon subsistence crises, but rather on the steady reproduction of generations larger than Ireland seemed capable of feeding or employing. Both short-term and cyclical fluctuations became ever less significant by comparison with the inexorable mechanism by which emigration generated further emigration.

Throughout the post-Famine century, emigration represented an expected stage in the cycle of life — the Irish equivalent of moving out of the parental household into lodgings in the modern city. Children were reared as potential emigrants, and when they reached adulthood many knew that they 'must travel'. With the increasing prevalence of impartible inheritance of land and 'stem family'* succession to household headship, only about one-third of the typical family of six children could hope to inherit or marry into land. Surplus children had therefore to migrate in search of marriage and employment. Since off-farm employment expanded only slowly, even contracting in parts of the north midlands, the bulk of each generation was pushed out of the country. The family push was strengthened by the growing dependence of those at home upon further 'American money' to subsidise the inefficient domestic economy. The decision to emigrate was thus made in a family rather than individual context, with parents and siblings contributing to the push and relatives already abroad to the pull. So long as the prospects of marriage and employment abroad remained markedly brighter than at home, most individuals gladly accepted the 'compensation' for waiving their claims which families urged upon them. Since these overseas prospects varied little according to one's regional or social origins, resistance to emigration was more likely to develop among more prosperous classes and in wealthier localities. This helps explain the heavier emigration rates from the west and the north midlands, by comparison with which Manchester or Boston seemed paved with gold. Emigration from poorer regions was further encouraged by the geographical coincidence of poverty and lack of non-agricultural employment. Yet everywhere in rural Ireland, though in varying degree, emigration was a practical and probable option when the parental household started to break up. Growing up in Ireland meant preparing oneself to leave it.

Part III: CONSEQUENCES

I'm very happy where I am
Far, far across the sea,
I'm very happy far from home,
In North Amerikay. [11]

Immigrant workers became an economic necessity in Britain and the New World during the nineteenth century. Less fastidious than the native-born, they were cheap, industrious, mobile and adaptable. Since most immigrants were young adults, the receiving economies benefited from acquisition of a labour force of 'instant adults' reared elsewhere. Immigration was essential to the rapid expansion of cities and industrial undertakings. Between about 1840 and 1910, the urban sector of the rapidly growing English population rose from 48 to 79 per cent, and that of the United States from 11 to 46 per cent. Natural increase and rural-urban migration alone could scarcely have generated this transformation. WILLIAMSON'S analysis indicates that if immigration to the United States had been halted between 1870 and 1910, population would have grown far more slowly, the industrial sector would have been less prominent, and average income would have been only slightly higher. Thus both the pace and shape of American economic development owed much to the immigration of foreigners ready to accept any job they could find.

The particular contribution of Irish immigrants to the economic transformation of receiving countries is more difficult to assess. America's rapid urban expansion at the middle of the century coincided with the heaviest influx from Ireland, and during the 1850s two-fifths of all foreign-born residents were Irish. But Irish immigrants played little part in the later phase of urban expansion around the turn of the century, and by 1910 only one foreigner in ten was Irish-born. A rough index of the numerical importance of the Irish migrant workers is obtainable from birthplace statistics for about 1870, which allow us to

31

compare the population born in Ireland with all those born outside their administrative unit of residence. The percentages Irish
were 11 for Great Britain, 13 for the United States, 24 for
Australasia and 33 for Canada. If internal migrants were
excluded, these proportions would of course be higher. In each
destination the Irish constituted a major labour force, but their
numerical weight within the migratory population was even
greater in the British possessions than in the United States or
Britain itself.

Irish emigrants were unusually well tailored for the rôle of
servicing other people's industrial revolutions. Rural background
and lack of skills did not impair their utility as labourers or
servants in foreign cities, and as construction workers or miners
outside the cities. Irish settlers in the United States were
consistently over-represented in these occupational categories,
by comparison with other immigrant groups as well as the native-
born. Ireland's abnormally heavy female emigration ensured that
American domestic service would become very much an Irish
domain, making a mockery of the old sneer that 'no Irish need
apply'. Irish emigrants, particularly those from Ulster to New
England, were also prominent in the textiles industry, one
sector in which skills were exported. Textiles skills were also
exported to certain British cities such as Bradford and Dundee.
But agricultural skills were seldom exploited abroad, partly
because spade cultivation was of little use in the prairies. In the
United States no immigrant group was so disinclined to work
in agriculture as the expatriate Irish. In various degrees Irish
settlers in other countries were also over-represented in the
humble but essential service occupations. Predominance of
young unmarried adults, the even balance of sexes, and low
expectations of comfort combined to render newly-arrived Irish
settlers model industrial proletarians.

Given their occupations, it is not surprising that Irish
emigrants to Britain and the United States tended to cluster in
urban districts and in slums within urban districts. Contrary to
myth, they did not congregate in Irish 'ghettos' to the exclusion
of other ethnic groups. Even the most notorious 'Irishtowns' of
foreign cities were of mixed ethnicity, though often of unmixed

class. Another myth would have it that the 'vast majority' of Irish emigrants invariably settled in major cities. This was true of the Irish in Britain by 1851, and in the United States by the end of the century. Yet America, as we have seen, was over- whelmingly rural during most of the century, only surpassing Ireland itself in urbanization in about 1860. Even in 1870, less than two-fifths of Irish-Americans were living in cities of over fifty thousand people. In the rural state of Iowa agriculture occupied more than half the Irish population. But the Irish were always abnormally inclined to cluster in what towns there were, and to avoid rural occupations even in rural regions. The great 'Irish' cities abroad were New York, Philadelphia, Boston and Chicago in the United States, and Liverpool, Glasgow, Manchester and London in Britain. For some decades New York had the largest Irish-born population of any city except Dublin.

In each country of settlement the Irish tended to settle not only in towns but in particular regions. In the Unites States they were more prone than other immigrant peoples to settle in eastern states, particularly in New England and New York. The geographical distribution of Irish-Americans (as a component of the foreign-born population) varied remarkably little between 1850 and 1910, reflecting not merely American industrial geography but also the constriction imposed by the emigration chain. The distribution of Irish settlers in Britain was also stable over time, as LAWTON has shown. Marked regional clusters developed by comparison with other migrant groups, the characteristically 'Irish' regions being south-west Scotland and England north of the Mersey.

The stability of settlement patterns among the Irish overseas masked intensive geographical mobility on the part of countless individual settlers. Many urban studies have shown that the working populations of British and American cities were highly mobile, shifting from lodging to lodging and from town to town within well-defined circuits. The ninetenth-century proletarian was highly responsive to fluctuations in income and employment levels, not least because he often found himself out of a job. The 'uprooted' immigrant was more responsive to differential pushes and pulls than most others. Irish seasonal workers in

Britain were noted for their economic pragmatism, as they followed the harvest and construction calendar about the British Isles in search of work. In the United States, Irish settlers seem to have been more sensitive than many other ethnic groups to regional economic disparities. Irish emigrants might be restricted to the worst jobs, but they clustered in regions of expanding employment. In effect, they occupied the worst seats in the best theatres.

Let us return to the example of Owen Mangan, whom we left in Philadelphia in 1869. Mangan's first American move was to join his brothers and train as a cooper, but in his impatience to save the fares for his family in England, he soon tried working in a woollen mill and also touching his American connections. But his aunt explained to him that 'every tub had to stand on its own bottom in this country', a response which 'settled me with my relations'. Mangan was about to take employment in an hotel when one of his chums from Preston persuaded him that work was to be had at Fall River, Massachusetts. As BERTHOFF shows, the path from 'the spindles and shuttles of Preston and Oldham' to Fall River was a common one, particularly among Irish expatriates. Mangan declined invitations from 'the boys' to join them in an Irish tenement, instead obeying the summons of an 'old friend' to operate looms at Ashton, Rhode Island. Despite the arrival of his family, Mangan's next twenty years were spent in restless mobility between these two states. He tried his hand as a travelling butcher, drugstore keeper, dry goods merchant and assistant, even shoemaker, often making several attempts at mastering each occupation. His final employment, characteristically peripatetic, was that of an insurance agent. Mangan's case illustrates the energy, opportunism and also rootlessness of the Irish 'exile', who often found it easier to acquire a job than an enduring home in his new country.

Social mobility was harder to accomplish than geographical movement. Mangan was earning eighteen dollars a week as a store assistant in 1891, only three dollars more than the wage he had rejected twenty years earlier as an hotel worker. What individual mobility there was tended to lie within the range of unskilled and semi-skilled service together with lower-grade clerical work. For women, marriage offered the only likely ladder. Irish girls were well placed to find partners outside their ethnic group because of the scarcity of other immigrant women. Much intermarriage with other ethnic and religious categories took place, but most partners were probably drawn from similar social classes. At least among the Boston Irish, upward mobility was largely restricted to the second generation. American-born Irishmen, like other settlers' children, were likely to achieve higher occupational status than their fathers, yet in aggregate they failed to bridge the initial gulf between Irish and other immigrant groups. By the turn of the century, however, the relative status of both fathers and sons had been raised by contrast with the influx of southern and central Europeans, who now occupied the bottom rungs once dominated by the Irish. The effect of this new influx of cheap labour was at once to raise the relative status of Irish workers already in the United States, and to lower the job chances of those planning to join them. Many occupations, particularly in agriculture and the professions, remained virtually free of Irish penetration. The Irish settler's principal, if contracting, rôle long remained that of servicing industrial expansion.

The partial exclusion of Irish immigrants from the societies which they served naturally encouraged cultivation of ethnicity, in defensive alliance against richer and often hostile host populations. Ethnic defensiveness was manifested in settlement patterns, marriage choices, political and social networks, religious participation, drinking practices, and persistent involvement in Irish affairs. More than other immigrant peoples to the United States, the Irish contributed men, plans and above all cash to home organisations, as well as subsidizing the domestic economy through remittances. Yet the concept of Irish 'community' in America or Britain is elusive. Emigrants often retained close links with their families at home while avoiding organised involvement with their fellow-countrymen abroad. Abundant evidence of self-consciously 'Irish' affiliations obscures the fact that vast numbers of emigrants quickly dropped out of ethnic networks, or exploited them only as a transitory tool for self-advancement. Most Irish-Americans probably did not read Irish newspapers, join Irish clubs, subscribe to Irish causes, or even wear shamrocks on St. Patrick's Day. But the active minority has dominated study of the Irish overseas, partly because evidence of non-involvement is negative, dull, and impossible to aggregate. It is fact that most Irish settlers were excluded from the most desirable houses, jobs and clubs; it is supposition that most of those excluded chose ethnic solidarity as their strategy for escaping alienation.

The Irish experience outside the British Isles and the United States was very different. Overall, the distinctiveness of Irish settlement patterns was closely associated with the numerical importance of the Irish component of each population. Countries like England and the United States as a whole had fairly small Irish proportions and relatively well-entrenched native-born majorities. Here the Irish were least likely to settle in regions dominated by farming or by native 'establishments'. In Australasia and Ontario, where the Irish were numerically more significant and the native-born populations weaker, Irish settlers did not avoid regions with large rural or native-born sectors. They were also more uniformly distributed between districts, though even in the dominions some districts were commonly identified as 'Irish'. Even within cities, Irish 'segregation'* was less marked than in Britain or the United States. Australasian settlers also seem to have been more socially mobile, more inclined to intermarry with other ethnic or religious groups, and less inclined to belong to 'Irish' organisations. Elements of exclusion and deprivation existed, but the emigrant with the enterprise, funding or good fortune to travel beyond Ireland's urbanized periphery faced fewer impediments to self-betterment. This point was constantly made by compilers of emigrant handbooks eager to guide their readers away from cities of sin and deprivation. Yet their advice, if followed, would have been self-defeating. Only urban industry could absorb the vast outflow of European emigration, and the minority which chose the colonies prospered precisely because these remained inaccessible to the majority. That majority, despite its deprivations, tended to find better living conditions, more regular employment and better marriage chances in the developing city than in the decaying home context of rural Europe.

The consequences of emigration for those who stayed at home were almost as far-reaching as for those who left. By continually removing the 'surplus' population of the poorest counties, emigration naturally tended to raise mean income and mean duration of employment. But its benefits for those individuals who had not emigrated were not immediately obvious. Emigration from the poorest districts was seldom sufficient to eliminate rural 'underemployment', and wage levels for those actually employed rose only slowly and unevenly during the second half of the century. Pre-Famine emigration was widely held to have made no impact upon wages. To the small extent that emigrants would otherwise have paid rents or taxes, their departure should have diminished the mean income of *rentiers* and landlords. The major positive effects of emigration on home income occurred during and just after the Famine, when the exodus of cottiers and small holders enabled remaining farmers to augment their holdings and their production. But thereafter the number of rural households declined only slowly, and emigration served to avert worse congestion rather than facilitate consolidation. The fears of those who decried emigration as a palliative rather than a cure were confirmed.

Emigration had two less direct consequences for national income. Irish parents (and to an increasing extent Irish and British taxpayers) had to meet the rearing costs of those 'instant adults' who proved so beneficial to urban expansion abroad. These costs grew with the improvement in living standards and extension of primary education after the Famine. Statisticians, contemporary and modern, have been fond of quantifying the expenditure so wasted upon rearing emigrants. But the concept of net economic loss is based on the assumption that emigrants, had they stayed home, would have produced enough surplus during an Irish adulthood to repay their collective 'debt' to Irish society (see MOKYR and Ó GRÁDA's analysis). Given the high level of underemployment which persisted despite emigration, it seems likely that many emigrants would have remained a social charge, either upon the state or upon their relatives, had their egress been prevented. Restriction of fertility, rather than subsequent curtailment of emigration, might therefore be deemed the most prudent strategy for Irish adults. But this analysis neglects the Irish belief that children were assets rather than liabilities, their principal attraction being their potential munificence as future emigrants. Already in 1835, the majority of Irish parishes examined by Whately's Commission were in receipt of subsidies in the form of emigrant remittances apart from pre-paid tickets. This was especially true of Leinster and Ulster. Towards the end of the century numerous observers in western regions reported that these remittances were essential to the continued payment of rent and shop debts and to the maintenance of the old people, particularly in periods of recession. Quite recently, emigrant remittances seem to have reached two per cent of gross national income in the Republic, and similar figures probably applied in the last century. Rearing for emigration was thus a form of insurance, with the parent qualifying for a pension or lump payment from his grateful offspring, shortly after their emigration. A given emigrant might default, but this only encouraged parents to insure doubly by rearing extra potential emigrants.

The overall result of heavy and prolonged emigration was to mitigate the need for economic transformation after the Famine and so to preserve and reinforce archaic features of the Irish economy. It is true that the massive movement between 1846 and 1854 facilitated the reorganisation of estates, consolidation of farms, and redirection of agriculture towards an even greater preponderance of capital-intensive dry cattle production. But subsequent stabilization of land holding set limits to further structural change, and many farms remained 'uneconomic' and dependant for their survival upon emigrant remittances. A further effect of continuous depopulation was to reduce post-Famine Ireland's attractiveness as a field for investment, and so to make still more improbable the diffusion of industrial and urban expansion throughout Ireland. Depopulation did not in itself preclude subsequent industrialization, as shown by the vigorous growth of new industries in the Belfast region, despite the fact that every county in Ulster had lost population during the 1840s. But the ever-shrinking Irish market clearly deterred many potential investors, particularly in key sectors such as railway construction. Emigration thus tended to slow down the twin processes of agricultural and industrial 'modernization', and to enable the Famine-shocked survivors to maintain unexpectedly many elements of their former way of life.

Emigration had analogous consequences for Irish demography. Ireland's pre-Famine demography was remarkable in the context of rural Europe only for the high emigration rate: marriage age, 'celibacy'* proportions, marital fertility* and mortality all appear to have fallen within the normal ranges for northern Europe. A remarkable facet of post-Famine demography was that most of these characteristics changed so little while the demographic profile of the rest of Europe was transformed. More spectacular, however, was Ireland's unique experience of continuous depopulation, which was mainly due to still heavier emigration together with the growing avoidance of marriage. By the end of the century, the Irish were among the most 'celibate' as well as the most migratory of populations.

Several models of interaction between emigration and marriage avoidance have been postulated. The expectation of emigration may have discouraged home marriage; the rarity of home marriage may have facilitated emigration. Individuals bent upon raising their living standards may have chosen between the alternative strategies of emigrating in search of higher income, or avoiding the need to share their home income with hungry dependants by remaining unmarried. The first two factors help explain the timing of marriage and emigration but not their eventual probability, while the third relies upon a simplistic model whereby economic decisions were determined by individual rather than family or group interests (see KENNEDY for an elaboration of this thesis). More plausibly, perhaps, one might argue that from the Famine onwards emigration was generally considered the optimum strategy for those without prospect of inheriting the family plot. The general availability of the emigration outlet between 1846 and 1854 enabled the rural population to adopt a novel set of values. These were manifested in the 'stem-family'* system of succession, impartibility of land-holding, and the mechanism of the property 'match' which made these systems workable. For those remaining in Ireland, non-marriage signified not the triumph of self-interest but defeat: the 'celibate' had failed either to escape Irish restrictions or to qualify for an Irish match.

Far from being land-holders cannily husbanding assets instead of spouses, the unmarried adult population consisted largely of underproductive dependants returned at the census as 'servants', 'labourers' or 'assisting relatives'. Under the stem system the match was usually contracted in advance of the transfer of occupancy, and fathers were as loath to hand land to unmarried sons as women were to accept men without land. The increasing rarity of marriage in the rural east should therefore be attributed to the chilling combination of a rigid marriage system and a decreasingly attractive emigration market. Judged in terms of family rather than individual economy, emigration of a member generated shared benefits whereas continued non-marriage entailed shared costs. The rigidity and growing inefficiency of the post-Famine marriage system may be traced to the initial prevalence and subsequent curtailment of emigration, in turn.

The promise of future support from emigrant progeny was perhaps the major factor in sustaining marital fertility at a level which became abnormally high in the changing context of late nineteenth-century Europe. Marital fertility in Ireland seems to have changed little over the century, being generally close to the highest levels on record. There was, however, variation between counties, and by the last third of the century fertility was markedly higher in the counties of heavier emigration. This supports the notion that the economic attractiveness of children depended upon their potentiality to emigrate, though the mechanisms by which married easterners limited their fertility within marriage remain obscure.

Overall fertility levels were also affected by regional variation in the female age at marriage, and once again the counties of heavier emigration (together with the major cities) tended to produce the younger brides — a correlation which was to be gradually reversed during the twentieth century. Large families in emigration-prone counties were further encouraged by fairly low mortality levels. The combination of earlier marriage, higher fertility and lower mortality tended to augment the population of young adults in the west, and thus increase the pressure for further emigration. Yet even in regions where emigration was relatively sluggish, Irish families continued to rear far more children than their European counterparts. Emigration was a national rather than local episode in the life-cycle, and made possible the maintenance of an archaic demographic as well as economic system.

The imprint of emigration might be traced in every sector of Irish life. The 'safety-valve' acted to reduce tensions arising from competition for land or benefits within the family group, yet it also helped concentrate what tensions remained upon key transactions such as transfer of household headship, negotiation of the dowry, and allocation of financial compensation to non-inheritors. Thus emigration played a causal role in the changing intensity and character of disputation within the family. Its shadow also suffused politics, for the overseas Irish became indispensable contributors to each new nationalist movement, and often interfered at critical points with its conduct. When emigration was unexpectedly stopped, as during the American recession of the 1870s or the First World War, the resultant surplus of frustrated youths who had expected to escape Ireland contributed both manpower and indignation to populist organisations such as the Land League and Sinn Féin. Ireland without emigration would have been a radically different place by 1921. But so pervasive were the consequences of emigration that no persuasive counterfactual history can be devised.

The place of emigration in the Irish life-cycle is poignantly symbolised by the institution of the 'American wake', otherwise termed the live wake, parting spree, farewell supper, feast of departure, or (in prosaic Donegal) the American bottle night. The celebration of departure, and subsequent 'convoy' to railway station or port, had evident parallels with the Irish celebration of death and its attendant promise of future benefits for those still living. During the Famine ritual tended to be neglected, and embarkation was seldom marked by anything more contrived than the odd 'merry dance' to the bowing of a fiddler. But the post-Famine revival of decorum was manifested in the farewell to emigrants from Killaloe in 1852, when

> these warm-hearted and simple-minded people demeaned themselves entirely as if they had been shrouded in all the privacy of home, clinging to and kissing and embracing each other with the utmost ardour, calling out aloud, in broken tones, the endeared names of brother, sister, mother, sobbing and crying as if the very heart would burst, while the unheeded tears ran down from the red and swollen eyes literally in streams.[12]

By 1882, however, a change of tone was perceptible in the ceremony of farewell. In Galway, the philanthropist Tuke 'did not hear a single "wail" as we left the ship; but before we steamed out a multitude of hand-shakings and blessings were showered upon me, and three cheers rang across the bay'.[13] In Queenstown, as Fr. SHEEHAN observed with sorrow,

> the crowds on shore look with envy at the fortunate friends who are escaping. They no longer shout an everlasting farewell, but a ringing cheer, which is strengthened by the hope that when the letter and the passage-money arrive, they, too, will be able to leave this land of bondage.

As the impulse to emigrate altered from shove to tug to promotion, so the expression of farewell changed from casual to sorrowful to congratulatory. Emigration became a fact of life, a 'fashion', a 'fever'. As P. D. Murphy wrote in 1917 of 'the intending emigrant': 'You can tell him at a glance, for there is something in his appearance that betrays him. He is listless, restless, discontented. . . He has caught the fever that has depopulated the Irish countryside'.[14]

NOTES

1. Sir William R. Wills Wilde, *Ireland, Past and Present: The Land and the People* (Dublin, 1864), p. 40.
2. Undated ballad to the tune 'There's a good time coming', in WRIGHT, p. 103.
3. Undated ballad, in 'Answer to Erin's lovely home', in WRIGHT, p. 104.
4. O'Connell to *Devon Commission*, House of Common Papers (H.C.P.), 1845 (Cd. 657), XXI, Minute 1119/49.
5. Parnell to *Select Committee on Colonisation*, H.C.P., 1890 (354), XII, Minute 5524.
6. Hierarchy's statement of 5 August 1859, quoted by SCHRIER, p. 61; Hierarchy's statement of 5 July 1883, quoted in appendix to *Report of Select Committee on Colonisation*, loc. cit., p. 494.
7. Duggan to *Richmond Commission*, H.C.P., 1881 (C. 2778-I), XV, Minute 14,199.
8. Mangan, typescript memoirs (1912), National Library of Ireland, MS 22,462.
9. *Dr. Cahill on Irish Emigration* (Dublin, 1857), in Royal Irish Academy, Halliday Pamphlets, 535/26.
10. Quoted by GOULD (1979), p. 632.
11. 'The emigrant's farewell, for 1865', in *The New Emigrant Songster* (Dublin, n.d.), in British Library, 11,622.f.2(3.).
12. John Forbes, *Memorandums Made in Ireland* (London, 1853), I, p. 202.
13. J. H. Tuke, 'With the Emigrants', *Nineteenth Century*, XII (July 1882), 152.
14. P. D. Murphy, 'Village Characters', *Ireland's Own*, XXIX (1917), 343.

GLOSSARY

CELIBACY PROPORTION: The percentage of men or women aged 45-54 who had never been married, according to their census schedules.

COHORT DEPLETION: The percentage of people aged 5-24 at one census who had 'disappeared' from the group aged 15-34 a decade later. This index of net outward migration is sensitive to mortality, internal movement, reverse migration and mis-recording of age, yet in the Irish context it provides a reasonable estimate of emigration rates among the age-group most heavily affected.

EMIGRATION RATE: The ratio of persons leaving Irish ports, with the intention of settling 'permanently' overseas, to the population of the county or region affected. Prior to 1851, the criteria used for computing rates of gross outward migration (or levels, as in Figure 1) were somewhat different, and several parallel tabulations are available for later years.

MARITAL FERTILITY: The ratio of births to married women of child-bearing age, standardised according to the age distribution of a standard population of wives to allow comparisons over time and between regions.

NET MIGRATORY INFLOW: An indicator of movement into Irish counties emanating from other Irish counties, based upon birthplace returns in the census. Counties which contained more natives of other Irish counties than they had contributed natives to other Irish counties were deemed regions of N.M.I.

REVERSE MIGRATION: Gross migratory inflow into Ireland from overseas. GOULD (1980, i) has computed 'repatriant ratios' for various ethnic groups in the United States, being the ratio of those arriving in the U.S.A. between 1904-5 and 1910-11, to those leaving the U.S.A. between 1907-8 and 1913-14. The figures quoted in the text are based upon immigrant aliens arriving from a foreign country (outflow), and emigrant aliens leaving for that country together with the difference between non-emigrant aliens leaving and non-immigrant aliens arriving (reverse flow).

SEGREGATION: The extent to which persons of Irish or other birthplaces tended to cluster in certain states, regions or wards of settlement overseas. The index used here, which is analogous to the geographer's 'index of segregation', is the coefficient of variation of the proportions of each regional population born in Ireland.

STEM FAMILY: A model of the system whereby control of households and of property was transferred between generations (see ARENSBERG & KIMBALL). Typically, a single selected inheritor brought his wife into the parental household before the death of one or both parents, the marriage being a parentally-arranged 'match'. Before assuming household control, the inheritor would undertake to make provision for his parents and offer compensation to his siblings in the form of cash, training, board and lodging, or an emigrant passage.

SELECT BIBLIOGRAPHY

Most statistical statements in this essay are based upon the author's analyses of regional and temporal variation in various aspects of Irish migration. The basic statistical data will be found in reports and returns submitted to the House of Commons, many of which are conveniently assembled in the 'Emigration' series of parliamentary papers republished by the Irish University Press (Shannon, 1968-72). These should be supplemented by immigration statistics compiled in the United States, Australia and Canada. For surveys and abstracts of the available statistics, consult the following:

N. H. CARRIER and J. R. JEFFERY, *External Migration: A Study of the Available Statistics 1815-1950* (London, 1953).

Imre FERENCZI and Walter F. WILLCOX, *International Migrations*, 2 vols. (New York, 1929, 1931).

IRELAND, Commission on Emigration and Other Problems 1948-1954, *Reports* (Dublin, 1955).

W. E. VAUGHAN and A. J. FITZPATRICK, *Irish Historical Statistics: Population 1821-1971* (Dublin, 1978).

The reading list which follows is confined to major and wide-ranging studies of Irish migration between 1801 and 1921. It omits local and particular studies, accounts of earlier and later migrations, most contemporary tracts, studies of Irish culture overseas, general analyses of migration, and general accounts of Irish economic, demographic and social history. Readers wishing to study these fields might consult:

L. A. CLARKSON, 'The Writing of Irish Economic and Social History since 1968', *Economic History Review,* XXXIII, 1 (1980), 100-11.

David Noel DOYLE, 'The Regional Bibliography of Irish America, 1800-1930', *Irish Historical Studies,* XXIII, 91 (1983), 254-83.

Joseph LEE (ed.), *Irish Historiography 1970-1979* (Cork, 1981).

T. W. MOODY (ed.), *Irish Historiography 1936-70* (Dublin, 1971).

Reading List

William Forbes ADAMS, *Ireland and Irish Emigration to the New World from 1815 to the Famine* (New Haven, 1932)—still the major monograph in its field.

Donald Harman AKENSON, *The Irish in Ontario: a Study in Rural History* (Kingston and Montreal, 1984); *Being Had: Historians, Evidence, and the Irish in North America* (Ontario, 1985); *Small Differences: Irish Catholics and Irish Protestants, 1815-1922, an International Perspective* (Kingston and Montreal, 1988); *The Irish in New Zealand* (Wellington, 1990)—challenging orthodoxies derived from beliefs about Irish emigration to the United States by examing better-documented movements to other countries.

Conrad M. ARENSBERG and Solon T. KIMBALL, *Family and Community in Ireland* (rev. ed., Cambridge, Mass., 1968)— important analyses of social functions of emigration, based upon anthropological study of Clare in the 1930s.

Rowland Tappan BERTHOFF, *British Immigrants in Industrial America* (Cambridge, Mass., 1953)—a useful survey despite its focus upon Britain rather than Ireland.

R. D. Collison BLACK, *Economic Thought and the Irish Question 1817-1870* (Cambridge, 1960)—essential analysis of the interaction of theory and policy as to emigration.

Brenda COLLINS, 'Proto-industrialization and Pre-Famine Emigration', *Social History*, VII, 2 (May 1982), 127-46—impact of regional economic change on emigration patterns.

E. J. T. COLLINS, 'Migrant Labour in British Agriculture in the Nineteenth Century', *Economic History Review*, XXIX, 1 (1976), 38-59—positive account of Irish 'harvesters'.

K. H. CONNELL, *The Population of Ireland 1750-1845* (Oxford, 1950)— classic but flawed analysis, strangely negligent of emigration.

S. H. COUSENS, 'The Regional Variations in Emigration from Ireland between 1821 and 1841', *Transactions and Papers of the Institute of British Geographers*, XXXVII (1965), 15-30; 'The Regional Pattern of Emigration during the Great Irish Famine, 1846-51', *ibid.*, XXVIII (1960), 119-34; 'Regional Variations in Population Changes in Ireland, 1881-91', ibid., XXXIII (1963), 145-62; 'Emigration and Demographic Change in Ireland, 1851-1861', *Economic History Review*, XIV, 2 (1961), 275-88; 'The Regional Variations in Population Changes in Ireland, 1861-1881', *ibid.*, XVII, 2 (1964), 301-21; 'Population Trends in Ireland at the Beginning of the Twentieth Century', *Irish Geography*, V (1968), 387-401—intricate studies by a geographer, marred by special pleading and failure to apply consistent analyses to different periods.

Helen I. COWAN, *British Emigration to British North America* (rev. ed., Toronto, 1961).

A. Gordon DARROCH and Michael D. ORNSTEIN, 'Ethnicity and Occupational Structure in Canada in 1871', *Canadian Historical Review*, LXI, 3 (1980), 305-33—tabulations by ethnicity (not birth-place) using sample of 10,000 house-holds.

Lord DUFFERIN, *Irish Emigration and the Tenure of Land in Ireland* (London, 1867)—important and well-documented defence of landlords against charge of 'extermination'.

Bruce C. ELLIOTT, *Irish Migrants in the Canadas: A New Approach* (Kingston and Montreal, 1988)—the first serious attempt to trace a migratory group (Tipperary-Canadian Protestants) before, during and after migration.

Charlotte ERICKSON, 'Emigration from the British Isles to the United States of America in 1831', *Population Studies*, XXXV, 2 (1981), 175-98; *Emigration from Europe 1815-1914: Select Documents* (London, 1976)—useful data on Ireland by the author of a magnificent study of English emigrant letters which has as yet no Irish counterpart.

David FITZPATRICK, 'Irish Emigration in the Later Nineteenth Century', *Irish Historical Studies*, XXII, 86 (1980), 126-43; survey chapters on emigration and on the Irish in Britain, 1801-70, in W. E. Vaughan (ed.), *A New History of Ireland*, V (Oxford, 1989), 562-660.

J. D. GOULD, 'European Inter-continental Emigration 1815-1914', *Journal of European Economic History*, VIII, 3 (1979), 593-679; IX, 1 (1980), 41-112; IX, 2 (1980), 267-315—useful if diffuse comparative study, though unreliable on Irish emigration.

David GRIGG, Population Growth and Agrarian Change (Cambridge, 1980)—useful conspectus of 'overpopulation' concept, with section on Ireland under heading 'Malthus Justified'.

Marcus Lee HANSEN, *The Atlantic Migration 1607-1860* (Cambridge, Mass., 1940)—impressive synthesis using Irish newspaper sources, though marred by factual slips.

C. J. HOUSTON and W. J. SMYTH, 'The Irish Abroad: Better Questions through a Better Source, the Canadian Census', *Irish Geography*, XIII (1980), 1-19—religious breakdown, 1871.

H. S. IRVINE, 'Some Aspects of Passenger Traffic between Britain and Ireland, 1820-50', *Journal of Transport History*, IV, 4 (1960), 224-41.

J. H. JOHNSON, 'Harvest Migration from Nineteenth-Century Ireland', *Transactions and Papers of the Institute of British Geographers*, XLI (1967), 97-112; 'Population Movements in County Derry', *Proceedings of the Royal Irish Academy* (sec. C), LX (1959-60), 141-62—based on Ordnance Survey memoirs for 1834.

Stanley C. JOHNSON. *History of Emigration from the United Kingdom to North America, 1763-1912* (London, 1913)—perhaps the most useful of older monographs in its field.

G. R. C. KEEP, 'Official Opinion on Irish Emigration in the Later Nineteenth Century', *Irish Ecclesiastical Record*, LXXXI (1954), 412-21; 'Some Irish Opinion on Population and Emigration, 1851-1901', *ibid.*, LXXXIV (1955), 377-86—rather patchy surveys.

Robert E. KENNEDY, *The Irish: Emigration, Marriage, and Fertility* (Berkeley, 1973)—includes elaborate discussion of emigration patterns assuming that individual self-interest governed decisions; covers period since Famine, with only occasional reference to regional variation.

R. LAWTON, 'Irish Migration to England and Wales in the Mid-Nineteenth Century', *Irish Geography*, IV (1959), 35-54—includes study of Liverpool Irish in 1851.

Lynn H. LEES and John MODELL, "The Irish Countryman Urbanized', *Journal of Urban History*, III, 4 (1977), 391-408—comparison of London and Philadelphia, *circa* 1850.

Oliver MACDONAGH, *A Pattern of Government Growth 1800-60: The Passenger Acts and their Enforcement* (London, 1961); *Emigration in the Victorian Age* (Farnborough, 1973)—review articles with introduction; 'The Irish Catholic Clergy and Emigration during the Great Famine', *Irish Historical Studies*, V, 20 (1947), 287-302; 'Irish Emigration to the United States and the British colonies during the Famine', in R. Dudley Edwards and T. Desmond Williams (eds.), *The Great Famine* (Dublin, 1956), 317-88; 'The Irish Famine Emigration to the United States', *Perspectives in American History*, X (1976), 357-446—meticulous and wide-ranging studies soundly based in primary research.

R. B. MADGWICK, *Immigration into Eastern Australia 1788-1851* (London, 1937).

Kerby A. MILLER, *Emigrants and Exiles: Ireland and the Irish Exodus to North America* (New York and Oxford, 1985)—splendidly documented and provocative, if impressionistic, study using several thousand letters from emigrants.

Joel MOKYR, *Why Ireland Starved* (London, 1983)—a fascinating but tendentious and flawed 'quantitive and analytical history of the Irish economy, 1800-1850'.

Joel MOKYR and Cormac Ó GRÁDA, 'Emigration and Poverty in Pre-Famine Ireland', *Explorations in Economic History*, XIX, 4 (1982), 360-84—rather inconclusive analysis of costs of emigration in terms of 'quality', 'human capital' and rearing.

Patrick O'FARRELL, *Letters from Irish Australia* 1825-1929 (Sydney and Belfast, 1984); *The Irish in Australia* (Sydney, 1986)—erudite and quirky.

Cormac Ó GRÁDA, 'Seasonal Migration and Post-Famine Adjustment in the West of Ireland', *Studia Hibernica*, XIII (1973), 48-76; 'A Note on Nineteenth-Century Irish Emigration Statistics', *Population Studies*, XXIX, 1 (1975), 143-49; 'Some Aspects of Nineteenth-Century Irish Emigration', in L. M. Cullen and T. C. Smout (eds.), *Comparative Aspects of Scottish and Irish Economic and Social History* (Edinburgh, 1977), 65-73; 'Across the Briny Ocean: 'Some Thoughts on Irish Emigration to America, 1800-1850', in T. Devine and D. Dickson (eds.), *Ireland and Scotland* (Edinburgh, 1983), 118-30—important studies of the reliability and interpretation of migration statistics, critical of Cousens.

C. H. OLDHAM, 'Incidence of Emigration on Town and Country Life in Ireland', *Journal of the Statistical and Social Inquiry Society of Ireland*, XIII (1914), 207-18—lively and penetrating analysis of interaction between emigration, demography and economic structure, stressing importance of excess female emigration.

M. A. G. Ó TUATHAIGH, 'The Irish in Nineteenth-Century Britain: Problems of Integration', *Transactions of the Royal Historical Society*, XXXI (1981), 149-73—skilful survey.

E. G. RAVENSTEIN, 'The Laws of Migration', *Journal of the Royal Statistical Society*, XLVIII, 2 (1885), 167-227; LII, 2 (1889), 241-301—classic postulation of 'laws' backed up by analysis of birthplace statistics including those relating to the Irish.

Arthur REDFORD, *Labour Migration in England 1800-1850* (rev. ed., Manchester, 1964)—two chapters on Irish influx.

Arnold SCHRIER, *Ireland and the American Emigration 1850-1900* (Minneapolis, 1958)—fascinating analysis of opinion, beliefs and ceremonial relating to emigration, drawing upon emigrant letters, folklore enquiries and press reports.

P. A. SHEEHAN, 'The Effect of Emigration on the Irish Churches', *Irish Ecclesiastical Record*, III (1882), 602-15—startling analysis of costs and benefits of emigration to the Catholic church.

Philip TAYLOR, *The Distant Magnet: European Emigration to the United States* (London, 1971)—best of several surveys of the character and process of transatlantic emigration.

Brinley THOMAS, *Migration and Economic Growth* (rev. ed., Cambridge, 1973)—quirky, disorderly but stimulating study of interaction of transatlantic business cycles and emigration, with much statistical analysis of the Irish movement to the United States.

Jacques VERRIÈRE, *La Population de l'Irlande* (Paris, 1979)—ingenious statistical manipulations to generate probability indices of emigration; much historical as well as contemporary analysis, marred by disorderly presentation and some careless argument.

Jeffrey G. WILLIAMSON, 'Migration to the New World: Long-term Influences and Impact', *Explorations in Economic History*, XI, 4 (1974), 357-89—counterfactual account of United States economic growth (1817-1913) without European immigration, using general equilibrium model.

Robert L. WRIGHT, *Irish Emigrant Ballads and Songs* (Bowling Green, Ohio, 1975)—vast collection, largely concerning emigration to America, with long but inaccurate bibliography.